The Way of Everything

of

(Tao Te Ching / 道德經)

Dedications:

I dedicate this book to my daughter, Amelie, alongside my parents and siblings. I thank them for "Everything" and in turn I thank "Everything" for them.

Legal Information:

Contents:

Introduction

The Tao Te Ching is a book of ancient wisdom which is said to have been written by a wise man named Laozi around 400-600 BC.

The author's true origins remain shrouded in the mysteries of time.

Vague records point to him being a wandering hermit, a skilled teacher, a philosopher, and some even speculate he was a keen astrologer.

Whatever he did in life, it is widely agreed he was someone revered by those who lived and worked with him in China.

Legend has it that around the age of eighty, he moved away from his home to seek the spiritual solitude of the countryside. Whilst journeying westward he is said to have been recognised and asked to write a book that captured his teachings on reason and virtue.

Regardless of whether this fabled history is accurate or not, the essence of the Tao Te Ching's wisdom is to benefit others.

Today the ancient book is still being used as a conduit for people to share their understanding of its content in a way that enhances lives.

The test of time is showing how the meaning of the text can progress and maintain its original good intentions.

Initially written in two parts called the "Tao Ching" and the "Te Ching", I decided to do the same with this book.

Some historians speculate that Laozi's second part was edited and added to during its first one hundred years. Such speculation does not matter.

People understand that words which respect and improve life should be revered no matter who writes them, or when they are written.

It is up to you to apply the wisdom you read to your own circumstances, ideally maintaining a constant intention to interpret the words in a way that gives you inner peace and helps you to be a good person.

I have read many versions of the Tao Te Ching and the authors who have inspired me the most are: Wayne Dyer, Deng Ming-Dao, Stephen Mitchell, Thomas Cleary, Ursula K. Le Guin, John Minford, Paul Carus, Jane English and Gia-Fu Feng.

Influenced by all of the translations I have read, I wanted to make my contemporary version unique whilst retaining the ancient book's original symbolism and meaning.

Short headings have been added to each chapter to help you reference and remember them more easily. Note, they are not intended to be the exact headings Laozi used.

The title of this book (The Way of Everything) is a modernised version of the original title (Tao Te Ching) which loosely translated means: The Book of the Way and Its Virtue.

Many translate the *Tao* to mean the *Way*. However, what we are trying to name cannot be named. With this in mind, I decided to intertwine the word *Everything* with the word *Way* throughout this book.

Used in conjunction with each other, these two words better describe the *oneness* of the Way.

Ultimately, my version was written with one intention. To subtly modernise Laozi's ancient wisdom to be easier to understand and apply to your daily experiences.

After countless rewrites, I believe my interpretation of the original text has achieved what it set out to do.

I hope the wisdom you read helps you find the answers you seek.

Kindly,
CJB

Tao Ching / 道經

Book 1

1. The Way

If you try to make sense of the Way
it will become nonsensical.

If you try to label the Way
the label will peel off.

The unnamed Way is where
unknown answers are hidden.

The named Way is where
known answers are found.

Therefore, in the unknown
lies unlimited spirituality,
and in the known
lies the limits of the physical.

Together the spiritual
and the physical flow
from the same mystery,
and this mystery of everything
is also part of the Way.

2. Flow

When people become
obsessed with beauty
their ugliness appears.

When people become
obsessed with perfection
their imperfection appears.

Everything has an opposite side
which together makes
everything whole.

Therefore, the wise act in silence
to let their actions speak,
and they go with the flow
to feel at one with the Way.

3. Worthiness

Highlighting the act of worthiness
causes its beneficial effect to fade.

Valuing something too much
can create costly problems.

Avoiding objects of temptation
will stop you yearning for them.

The wise ensure others feel worthy
for who they are within
and they focus them
on what is important
to remain strong.

Most importantly
they do nothing
when there is
nothing to do.

4. Love

The Way is mostly invisible
to the human eye.

Its invisibility is what
makes it indefinitely useful.

The Way is without shape
yet it gives rise to many forms.

The Way naturally flattens
that which protrudes.

The Way naturally releases
that which is trapped.

The Way naturally deflects
attention away from itself
and is part of everything,
even dust.

→

The Way does all this in peace
and like a mother
it nurtures everything
with love.

5. Centred

The Way does not favour
one thing over another.

The Way does not
plan, plot or side.

The Way fills all empty spaces
by emptying all filled spaces.

To stay centred
you must know
when to speak
and when to keep silent.

6. Mother

Everything benefits
from a mother,
especially one
who is patient
and embodies
the mysterious qualities
of heaven and earth.

The motherly Way
dwells within your spirit
and without effort,
its love remains
forever yours.

7. Logic

The Way cannot end
because it never began.

It can never be wrong
because it never needs to be right.

The wise know to copy this logic
and in doing so they become one
with everything they do.

8. Goodness

Water and goodness are akin.
Without them, things cannot thrive.
Permeating all things without motive
they become level, and by being soft
they experience no resistance.

Within you lies infinite goodness
which will always guide you
to do the right thing.

Let goodness flow
through your actions
and they will be respected.

9. Proud

Things which require
constant action
stop you from
achieving them
via non-action.

Things which require
too much attention
will eventually
blur your focus.

Surrounding yourself
with riches
makes you feel
less secure.

Be silently proud
of accomplishments
and others will
notice them.

10. Virtuous

Remain whole
by accepting
the physical
and spiritual
are one.

Remain young
by using
energy wisely
and being supple.

Remain pure
through self-awareness,
and let unconditional love
unite those around you.

Let the light of the Way
filter through you
to help others
without you knowing.

→

The wise encourage
and nurture others
to become productive,
and do so
without assertion.

The virtuous help people up
when they are down,
and do so
without conditions.

11. Space

The spokes of a wheel
unite at the centre, yet
it is the surrounding space
that makes them useful.

Solid forms are made useful
by utilising the empty spaces
inside and outside of
their design.

External walls and windows
form a house, yet
it is the internal space
that turns the house
into a usable home.

Therefore, physical forms
only function because
the space of non-existence
makes them functional.

12. Distractions

A rainbow makes it hard
to see one colour.

Noise makes it hard
to hear one sound.

Succulence spoils
the flavour.

Overindulgence leads
to madness.

Hard to reach riches
keeps them at arm's length.

Thus, the wise look
for inner guidance
when the outer world
causes unwanted distractions.

13. Fear

Fame and rejection
are like fear
because both
can make you
feel anxious.

Fame raises you
to new social heights;
hence the threat of losing it
can seem like a huge fall.
Together these extremes
make you fearful.

Yet it is only
your physical body
that can hold fear,
as without it
where would such
feelings manifest?

→

Hence the wise
treat others
as they would
themselves.

This means others
do not fear
to be treated
by the wise.

With this knowledge,
the wise remain brave.

With this knowledge,
the wise remain carefree.

With this knowledge,
the environment remains calm.

14. Abstruse

Although the Way
is everywhere
it is transparent.

Although it speaks
many cannot hear it.

Try to grab it
and it will elude you.

These united discrepancies
make the Way what it is.

Its presence is not clear.
Its absence is not obscure.
Names cannot describe it.

→

The Way simply is what it is
and does what it does
and with and without form,
having image and non-image,
it stays wonderfully abstruse.

With no sides to enter
you are already within it.

Knowing all this the wise
respect their past
by staying present
and accepting
they are part
of the whole.

15. Ancestors

Long ago lived the wisest
of the ancestors.

Their subtle, spiritual, profound
and penetrating teachings were
beyond the comprehension
of the ignorant.

To begin to understand
these ancestors
you must first
accept they were
reluctant,
reserved,
elusive,
simple,
empty
and obscure.

→

In behaving this way,
they could do
the impossible.

They could make the angry
eternally pacified.

They could spur to life
those who were still.

To become as wise as these ancestors
you should never seek or want,
as only then can you never
want what you seek.

16. Eternal

Stop thinking and
you will find peace.

Stop moving and
peace becomes eternal.

Nature is recognised by
its cycles of movement
and stillness.

Knowing you are
destined for
eternal peace
leads to enlightenment,
not knowing this
leads to the opposite.

The wise have no fear
because they know
the death of their body
is merely the continuation
of their eternal journey.

17. Leadership

Those who
are led well
do not know
they were led.

Those who
attach themselves
to their leader
praise them.

Those who
fear their leader
despise them.

Those who
have no faith
in their leader
will not be led,
and with no faith,
they will not listen.

→

Leaders who have gained merit
from their accomplishments
make those they led
feel they were part
of their success.

18. Trouble

When all seems lost,
morality and kindness
can guide you.

When over-cautious
and condescending,
hypocrisy can blind you.

When rebellion appears,
family loyalties can be tested.

When everyone is in trouble,
solutions rely on collaboration.

19. Harmony

In the absence of
arrogance and
condescension,
people will
thrive.

In the absence of
taking the moral
high ground
people will not
feel low.

In the absence of
displaying wealth
people will not
be tempted.

These three absences
will lead to
harmony.

20. Nourishment

Those who clear
their mind
notice their
anxieties
clear too.

Those who
say yes and
don't mean it
are different
from those who
say yes and do.

Those who
take good actions
differ from
those who
take bad ones.

→

Those who
are fearful
are only afraid
of fear itself,
and the worst
that can be dreamt
never transpires.

Those who
take joy
for granted
are unprepared,
hence they
are saddened
when joy ends.

Those who
stay calm and innocent
remain as guilt-free
as the day
they were born.

→

Those who
have too much
often feel
unfulfilled.

Those who
are ignorant
stay blinded
until they open
their eyes
to wisdom.

Those who
are trapped
in their mind
do not experience
the joys of
freedom.

Those who
are wise
need nothing
but the nourishment
of the Way
to sustain them.

21. Essence

The Way holds
endless virtuosity
without being virtuous.

It is ever moving,
hence remains elusive.

It reveals distinct forms and yet
they remain obscure.

The Way is limitless
in what it can hold,
yet it does not hold
anything,
and by not holding
anything,
it shows its essence.

→

The Way has been
what it is
since it was
what it isn't.

It has never changed
because it does not have to.

How do we know all this?
Because we cannot know.

22. Whole

The broken can be mended.
The bent can be straightened.
The empty can be filled.
The tired can be motivated.
The low can be made high.

Therefore, the wise
embrace unity
and in doing so
they become
a model for
others.

They remain humble
and thus demonstrate
their enlightenment.

The wise do not need
to be assertive, hence
they remain distinguished.

→

By not bragging,
their merit grows.

By not seeking approval,
their intent lasts.

By not competing,
they have no opponents.

By behaving this way,
they feel whole.

23. Succumb

Peace is a part of nature
and turmoil will always
succumb to it.

Hence the wise
act with reason
to calm those who
are unreasonable.

They act with morality
to guide those who
are immoral.

They act accepting loss
is a part of winning.

They act in faith
to teach
the unfaithful.

24. Misshapen

You cannot stand firm
whilst tiptoeing
and you cannot walk
without moving your legs.

Highlighting your strengths
weakens them.

Boasting dims the results
of your actions.

Approving your conduct
can lead to misconduct.

Praising yourself too highly
will stop you from growing.

→

If you go against the Way
you will become misshapen,
and by being misshapen
you will not fit into the world
as well as you could.

Flow with the Way
and the Way will flow
with you...

25. Everything

Before everything,
there was still
everything.

During everything,
there is still
everything.

After everything,
there will still be
everything.

As the Way is an
unnameable word for
everything,
it flows through time
without being subject to time.

→

It has been said that
the Way is great,
hence everything is great,
such as:

- all beings,
- all planets,
- all universes.

The Way naturally
takes care of
these three things
alongside everything else,
therefore, everything else
should do the same.

26. Serendipity

Heaviness is not known
without lightness.

Movement is not known
without stillness.

Hence the wise accept
their daily troubles,
knowing they will be
countered by serendipity.

They know excess
can lead to limitations,
and reacting hastily
can lead to the loss
of something.

27. Duty

Those who
walk their path well
leave no trace.

Those who
speak well
make no errors.

Those who
calculate well
do so without assistance.

Those who
make the perfect lock
do so without needing a key
to unlock it.

→

Those who
connect things seamlessly
do so without needing bonds,
hence those things
remain connected.

The wise always use goodness
to help other forms,
no matter who
or what they are,
and in doing so
they spread enlightenment
without assertion.

It is the duty of the wise
to teach others how good
overpowers bad.

It is the duty
of those who do bad,
to learn how to be good.

28. Equality

Balancing masculinity
with femininity
is what enables
the wise
to always
be at their best.

Being at their best
is what makes
the wise
and others
feel good.

Knowing dark and light
are equally needed
is what keeps
the world balanced.

→

Keeping the world balanced
unleashes its potential.

Knowing success and failure
are equally needed
is what keeps
the world at peace.

Keeping the world at peace
is what makes
life simple.

Embodying the simplicity
of natural equality
is the greatest kindness
you can give
to the world.

29. Sparsely

Try to make
and control
everything
and you will fail.

Everything forms
the divinity
of the Way.

Therefore, the Way cannot
be made or controlled,
attempting to do so will
mar any expectations.

Try to hold onto everything
and everything will slip
through your grasp.

→

The world has so many
struggling people
because they are
each trying to hold on to
too many things.

The wise know the path
to feeling uplifted is to
live sparsely so that
nothing heavy can
weigh them down.

30. Peace

Leaders should set
good examples
for others to follow
and then
if war arises
peace is sought.

Aggression will lead
others to harm,
and harm will lead
others to aggression.

By all means, lead others,
but lead them towards:
peace,
unity,
harmony,
acceptance
and tolerance.

$\rightarrow$

Remember the Way
is everything
and everything is you.
Hence hurting others
will hurt you too.

Peace can never involve conflict
as conflict weakens all involved.

A successful and wise leader
knows all this, hence leads
by following the Way.

31. Warrior

A fighter uses tools
to harm.

A warrior uses tools
to heal.

A fighter battles
to create unrest.

A warrior defends
to create rest (peace).

A fighter does not see
those he fights as human.

A warrior knows
all fighters are human
and will avoid a fight.

→

A fighter gets covered
in the blood of others.

A warrior stays clean
by avoiding the
loss of blood.

A fighter celebrates
the conquering
of others.

A warrior avoids
conquering others
to be able
to celebrate.

A fighter
never wins.

A warrior
always wins.

32. Simplicity

The eternal nature
of the Way
cannot be named.

Its simple nature
cannot be contained.

Complex situations
seek simplicity.

Everything
seeks simplicity.

The physical
and non-physical
thrive in simplicity.

→

This being known,
the wise seek
a simple life
by following
the Way.

Seeking the simple life
brings them safety
and comfort.

It is simplicity that
makes the Way flow
like a stream into a river
and a river into
a vast ocean.

33. Overcome

Knowing how
others will react
is wisdom.

Knowing how
you will react
is also wisdom.

A wise person
can overcome
others and themselves.

Being aware
what you have
is enough,
is enough to
make you realise
you are naturally wealthy.

→

Understanding
everything cannot die
is to understand
there is no
life and death.

The Way
is what it is
and always will be.

34. Greatness

The greatness
of the Way
flows through
everything,
and everything
succumbs to
its flow.

The greatness
of the Way
influences
everything,
and everything
remains unaware.

Everything comes
from its greatness,
and everything
returns to it.

→

The Way has
no control,
which is why
it is truly great.

35. Desire

Everything is
attracted to those
who follow the Way
because everything
naturally seeks serenity
and contentment.

The unwise are
attracted to the
wrong things
through visual desire,
hence lose sight of
the invisible Way,
especially as it
does not compete
and has no lure.

→

Unwise people
still feel empty
even when their
desire is fulfilled.

It is only those
who flow
with the Way
who can feel
forever fulfilled.

36. Nature

To reduce what is powerful,
learn how it is induced.

To weaken what is powerful,
learn how it is strengthened.

To withdraw what is powerful,
learn how it is given.

Such simple rules come from
the all-powerful balance of nature
therefore, it is wise to learn
you cannot have one thing
without the other.

With this knowledge, show
tenderness to those
who are harsh
and peace
will stay
in its place.

37. Passive

The Way is
passive by nature,
and yet by nature,
it gets things done.

If leaders embraced the Way,
nations would also get things done.

If people reverted to nature
there would be no desire
for more and more,
as less and less
would be needed.

A passive world is a
peaceful world.

Te Ching / 德經

Book 2

38. Choices

A truly good act
is done selflessly.

A truly bad act
is done selfishly.

Good acts
need no effort
to get things done.

Bad acts
need huge effort
and get nothing done.

Kindness is doing nothing
when nothing will help.

Unkindness is doing something
when nothing will help.

→

Those who forcefully
preach loyalty and faith
end up weakening
their message and
create turmoil.

Hence, it is wise:

To stay
in the solidity
of each moment.

To focus on
what you have
rather than what
you have not.

To find
contentment
by making the
right choices.

39. Unity

Unity creates
the Way
and the Way
creates unity.

United things
become clear.

United things
become peaceful.

United atoms
form the mind.

United valleys
form the earth.

United energies
form life.

→

United people
form nations.

Therefore, without unity:

The Way would not
be seen as one.

The mind would not
be heard by one.

The earth would not
hold together as one.

Interfering with unity
will pollute the sky,
water and land,
and all beings
and their spirits
will suffer.

→

This is why people
must stand united,
to instigate
a united environment,
to understand
cause and effect,
to be humble and balanced.

Success should not
be measured by
individual achievements
if those achievements
do not unite.

40. Always

The Way
always returns.

The Way
always yields.

The Way
embodies existence
and non-existence
hence it will
always remain.

41. Revealed

When the Way
is revealed
to wise people,
they embody it.

When the Way
is revealed
to the less wise,
they only use
parts of it.

When the Way
is revealed
to the ignorant,
they mock it,
and their mocking
validates its wisdom.

→

The lessons
to be learnt
are:

The way
to enlightenment
can be dark.

The way
forward
may involve
stepping back.

The way
can seem long
if no steps
are taken
at all.

The way
to great power
comes from
being powerless.

→

The way
to purity is
not always clear.

The way
to unconditional love
is to not make it
conditional.

The Way
is invisible
yet it can be felt
everywhere you go.

42. Destruction

The Way flows
from one,
to two,
to three,
and so on.

The Way flows
from non-being
into being
and so on.

The Way consists
of yin and yang
and together
they harmonise.

Pull yin and yang apart
and you cause destruction.
This is a lesson to be heeded.

43. Lesson

Flexibility can
overcome
any hardship.

The formless
can enter
what is not yet
formed.

Learning to
not say and do
what must be done
is what helps it
to be achieved.

This is a lesson
only a few
can master.

44. Control

Label or form,
which is more meaningful?

Health or wealth,
which is more valuable?

Gain or loss,
which is more heartfelt?

Obsession wastes
much time
and energy.

Obsessively
collecting things
will heighten
the pain felt
when you lose
what has been
collected.

→

Accept
what you
have happily,
then others
will accept you
happily too.

Those who
can control
themselves
avoid being
endangered.

Those who survive
will live to enjoy
another day.

45. Understand

In im**perfection,**
you will always find
perfection.

Fullness can only
be valued once
it is emptied.

The straighter something is,
the more it appears crooked.

The sharper something is,
the more brittle it will seem.

The more you repeat eloquent words,
the more their effect wanes.

Move when you are cold.
Stay still when you are hot.

→

You will always find
peace and clarity
if you understand
the nature of things.

46. Need

When people
listen to
the Way
no badness
needs
to be done.

When people
do not
listen to
the Way
much goodness
needs
to be done.

Greed destroys
the joy of attaining.

Power destroys
the joy of sharing.

→

If you can be content
with what you have,
you will have all
you ever need.

47. Seeking

In not seeking
and wanting,
you will find
the Way.

In not seeking
external joy,
internal joy
will appear.

The wise know
to think less
to feel more,
to understand less
to succeed where
others fail.

48. Achieve

A foolish mind focuses
on too many things
which leads
to stress.

A wise mind focuses
on one thing
which leads
to success.

By doing less
you achieve more.

To achieve goals,
you must
be patient.

Those who
are not patient
will fail.

49. Listen

The wise
do not impose
their thoughts
on others
unless asked
by others
to do so.

The wise
are kind
to everything
and that is
how we know
they are kind.

→

The wise
are trusting
of everything
and that is
how we know
they are trusting.

The wise
speak softly
so that others
come closer
to listen.

50. Journey

Life is a journey
that you
must take.

How you take it
is dependent on
your attitude.

If you have
a bad attitude,
bad things
will happen.

If you have
a good attitude,
good things
will happen.

Journey without fear
and fear will not
hinder you.

51. Freedom

Having a virtuous cause
encourages people
to live.

Kind acts ensure
people are
cared for.

Persistence
shapes people,
and health
sustains them.

Freedom to choose
the right path
is what leads
people to find
the Way.

52. Youthful

As the Way
is everything
and the world is part
of everything,
the Way is
the natural mother
of the world.

In accepting this truth
everything is revealed
as a united family,
and like any
united family,
kin will feel protected
throughout their lives.

Children who grow
into contented adults
will never be troubled.

→

Whereas children who grow
into discontented adults
will always feel troubled.

To recognise your limitations
is to be enlightened.

To remain youthful
is to remain strong.

Those who remain
enlightened and youthful
will be forever young.

53. Path

Humility keeps you
on the right path,
whereas arrogance
takes you off it.

The right path is
very clear to see,
yet people tend to
deviate from it.

When a nation's wealth
is spent only on the capital,
the whole country feels poor.

Extravagance creates
misery elsewhere
and is a path
best avoided.

54. Appreciate

With firm foundations,
you cannot be moved.

With constant protection,
you cannot be destroyed.

If individuals, families,
nations and the world
appreciate the Way,
goodness will
endure eternally.

Hence individuals who
appreciate the Way
help other individuals thrive.

Families who
appreciate the Way
help other families thrive.

→

Nations who
appreciate the Way
help other nations thrive.

Worlds who
appreciate the Way
help other worlds thrive.

The test of time
makes us appreciate
these natural truths.

55. Spirit

Embody the Way
and feel forever young.

Embody the Way
and poison cannot take effect.

Embody the Way
and anger cannot take hold.

Embody the Way
and predators cannot strike.

A child is supple
yet grows stronger each day.

A child is innocent
yet is full of energy.

A child cries
yet never loses their voice.

→

A child is in harmony
with nature.

To know the harmonious
is called eternal.

To know the eternal
is called enlightenment.

To watch life grow
is called a blessing.

A child's strength
comes from love,
and although
an adult body
eventually dies,
the spirit
of the child
remains eternal.

56. The Wise

The wise
do not preach,
hence those
who preach
are not
being wise.

The wise
control
their temper
to avoid
losing it.

The wise
untangle
the complex.

→

The wise
remain humble
to allow others
to shine.

The wise
stay grounded
to allow their wisdom
to take root.

The wise
are not misled
or corrupted,
and as a result
they help make
the world
a better place.

57. Thrive

For a nation
to thrive
it must
be given
freedom.

Controlling
communities
too tightly
strangles them.

Loosening control
enables people
to breathe freely.

Wrapping people
in red tape
causes them
to struggle.

→

Weighing people down
with heavy tools
makes them collapse.

Balance is the answer.

Cut the red tape
where it gets tangled.

Lighten the tools
and provide help
where it is needed.

Do all this
and a nation
and its people
will thrive.

58. Paradox

Rule a nation
with compassion
and its people will
act the same way.

Rule a nation
with a heavy hand
and its people will
feel bruised.

In finding
some happiness
you will face
sorrow.

In being honest
you will face
lies.

→

In being positive
you will face
negativity.

This is the eternal
paradox.

Hence a wise ruler
treats all sides
they face as
one.

In doing this they
avoid people
getting hurt.

In doing this they
can be forthright
yet seen to care.

In doing this they
can speak so
every word
is heard.

59. Balance

Balance is key
to good governance.

In balancing power,
you find harmony.

In balancing harmony,
you find power.

In balancing,
you centre yourself
in the Way.

By centring yourself
in the Way,
you feel supple,
strong and unlimited.

This is how roots last.

This is how to live.

60. Actions

Treat others
as you would
treat yourself.

Let your actions
always be good
so good will come
from your actions.

61. Harmony

When a nation
is truly powerful
its power becomes
the underpinning
of all countries
within it.

A powerful nation
should act
like a mother,
always caring
for its children,
no matter the cost.

→

A powerful nation
should know
the softness
of femininity
permeates
the hardness
of masculinity.

A powerful nation
should know
by remaining calm,
other countries
will allow it
to cradle them.

A powerful nation
should know
keeping low
creates stability,
keeping high
creates instability.

→

Hence, harmony
is achieved
by creating a nation
where people are
not afraid
to rise-up
or fall-down.

If a nation
can provide
such harmony
its reign
will be
eternal.

62. Honoured

The Way
is a place
of protection
for the rational.

The Way
is a place
of much value
for the good.

The Way
is a place
of karma,
guidance and
forgiveness
for the bad.

With rationale words,
one can therefore
protect.

→

With good actions,
one can therefore
achieve more
with others.

With bad actions,
one can therefore
choose to return
to being good.

The children of the Way
hear many stories of
its magnificence,
but its *stillness* is
the greatest story
of them all.

The wise know this.

→

They understand
that by remaining still,
magnificence comes to them,
and when they are most in need,
they will be guided by the Way.

For all these things
everything should
feel honoured.

63. Steps

Do less with more,
and do more with less.

Experience the bland
to improve your taste.

Master silence
to control life's noise.

See the weak as strong,
see the strong as weak,
and help both adjust.

Help sooner
rather than later,
or else it will be
too late to act.

Short steps
will take you far.

→

The wise take
small actions,
hence achieve
big results.

Underestimating tasks
makes them
more difficult.

Hence, the wise plan
for all eventualities
and are ready
to tackle them
one step at a time.

64. Guided

Those who are silent
are more easily guided.

Those who have not yet started
are more easily stopped.

Those who are weak
are more easily broken.

Those who are tiny
are more easily scattered.

See things
before they appear,
and arrange them
before they arrange
themselves.

→

Like a tree,
great things
start small.

Great structures
start with a
single brick.

Acting hastily
raises the odds
of failure.

Grabbing
leads to things
slipping away.

The wise are patient
to increase their odds
of success.

The wise do not
act rashly hence
remain in control.

→

Those who are
near the end
often return to
the beginning.

It is wise to
treat every step
of a journey
with caution.

If you have
no desire
you cannot
be tempted.

The wise
give back
to others
more than
they receive.

The wise
help others
find the Way
for themselves.

65. Distracted

Long ago
people respected
natural order,
hence the Way
did not need
to be taught.

Over time
the minds of people
were easily distracted
and the Way became
lost to them.

Thankfully the wise
never forgot the Way
hence were able to
help others to
find it again.

→

By remembering
the Way
you retain
both wisdom
and goodness.

By retaining
both wisdom
and goodness
you create firm
foundations for
you and others
to thrive.

By ignoring
both wisdom
and goodness
they will be
brought to
your attention
even more.

66. Perspective

Land is powerful
because it is
not afraid
to lower itself
to the other
forces of nature.

Therefore:

The wise who
lead from above
also support from below.

The wise who
offer sustenance know
to first provide nourishment.

→

The wise who
are prepared to take
the first blow,
will protect others.

The wise who
know to respect
every perspective
will rarely argue.

67. Karma

The Way's
extraordinariness
comes from its
ordinariness.

Those who
try to be extraordinary
but do not remain ordinary
will soon fade.

The wise know:

You must
be compassionate
to be brave.

You must
be prudent
to be generous.

→

You must
be respectful
to be respected.

To not be these
three things
triggers karma
and you will induce
the opposite qualities.

Be these
three things
and karma will
protect you.

68. Success

Successful warriors
do not wage war.

Successful combatants
are not easily provoked.

Successful champions
do not wish to confront others.

Successful entrepreneurs
produce what others need.

Successful leaders
inspire those who follow.

Successful people
embody the Way
because the Way
promotes success
without effort.

69. Compassion

Experienced warriors
wish to be friends,
not foes.

Experienced warriors
are not afraid to move
backwards.

Experienced warriors
never underestimate
their foes.

Experienced warriors
show compassion hence
they always win.

70. Follow

The Way makes things
simple to understand
and simple to follow.

Yet society makes things
complicated to understand
and even harder to follow.

The Way created
words for good.

The Way created
actions for good.

Misuse both and
their goodness
gets hidden.

→

Hence:

The wise
are impeccable
with their words.

The wise
are impeccable
with their actions.

The wise
are impeccable
with their love.

71. Ignorant

To understand
without being taught
is healthy.

To be ignorant
after being taught
is unhealthy.

It is only by
realising you
are ignorant
that you can
start to heal
yourself.

The wise dislike
being ignorant
hence remain healthy.

72. Respect

When people
lose respect
for each other
evil ensues.

Therefore,
set the example
and respect others
at home and at work.

Do not interfere
and just let others be.

In letting others be
you are teaching them
through non-action.

73. Outcomes

Recklessness
leads to high-risk
outcomes.

Cautiousness
leads to low-risk
outcomes.

Either
leads to good or bad
outcomes.

The Way
silently decides all
outcomes.

$\rightarrow$

The Way does not
need to speak
to have its
lessons
heard.

The Way does not
need summoning
as it is always
with you.

The Way is part of
everything.

You are part of
everything.

Therefore,
you can always
feel assured you
will be protected
by the Way.

74. Hurt

Those who are not
afraid of dying
cannot be
intimidated
with death.

Those who are not
fearful
cannot be
made
to fear.

If you go
against the Way
and threaten those
who cannot be threatened,
you will be the one
who gets hurt.

75. People

When people
cannot afford food,
they starve.

When people
are made to obey,
they learn to disobey.

When people
see death as an option,
they may choose it.

Therefore,
let people be
when they have
what they need.

76. Flexible

Young things are flexible
hence can be shaped easily.

Old things are stiff
hence can be broken easily.

To remain young,
remain flexible.

To remain old,
remain stiff.

Those who are flexible
let life shape them.

Those who are stiff
let death take them.

The flexible re-adjust,
whilst the stiff break apart.

77. Strength

The Way gets compared
to a tightly strung bow.

It naturally knows what
is above and below only
generates strength whilst
moving in the same
direction.

Society does the opposite,
it takes strength from the low
to give more to the high.

Therefore, the wise
help maintain balance
whenever they can
and expect nothing
in return.

78. Truth

Water is the
most powerful
force on earth.

Soft and dispersible
it penetrates and
wears away the
hardest of rocks.

Its power cannot
be disputed.

Nature has proven
the soft penetrates
the hard so that, over time,
the hard becomes soft.

People are aware
of this truth and yet
they seldom act on it.

→

Hence you should:

Show the hardened
some softness
and they will
eventually be soft.

Show the bad
some goodness
and they will
eventually be good.

This truth
can often seem
paradoxical.

79. Sweetness

Serious arguments
leave a bitter taste
in the mouths
of those involved.

However, the wise
accept you cannot
enjoy sweet things
unless you have
experienced
something bitter.

They know karma
eventually offers
sweetness to those
who remain
sweet-natured.

80. Happy

People are happy
when they feel protected
and do not feel the need
to protect themselves.

People are happy
when they have
vehicles and tools
and no need
to use them.

People are happy
when they can appreciate
life's simple pleasures
throughout a long
lifetime.

A community is happy
when neighbouring
communities are
happy too.

81. Wealth

Those who are truthful
are not always kind.

Those who are kind
are not always truthful.

Those who are wise
are not argumentative.

Those who are argumentative
are not wise.

Those with knowledge
may not know.

Those who know
may not have any knowledge.

→

If you give all you have
to others, nothing can be
taken from you.

The more you can help
the less you will hinder.

The more you give
the wealthier you will feel.

The Way is naturally
the wealthiest of us all,
as it keeps on helping
and it keeps on giving.

Printed in Great Britain
by Amazon